The Woodsman And His Hatchet

EIGHTY YEARS ON BACK COUNTRY SURVIVAL

The Woodsman And His Hatchet

EIGHTY YEARS ON BACK COUNTRY SURVIVAL

BUD CHEFF SR.

Author of "Indian Trails & Grizzly Tales"

ILLUSTRATIONS BY TERRY DORR

The Woodsman
And His Hatchet

EIGHTY YEARS ON BACK COUNTRY SURVIVAL

BUD CHEFF SR.

Published in the United States of America

ISBN 0-912299-62-2

STONEYDALE PRESS PUBLISHING COMPANY
523 Main Street • P.O. Box 188
Stevensville, Montana 59870
Phone: 406-777-2729

1-27-97 Stoneydale 12.95

Table of Contents

COVER PHOTO:
*Using nothing but basic tools and "survival" or "emergency" items he carries in his daybag, and utilizing a technique he describes in "**The Woodsman and His Hatchet,**" author Bud Cheff Sr. constructed this emergency shelter of natural materials in about a half an hour. Photo by Dale A. Burk.*

THE WOODSMAN AND HIS HATCHET: EIGHTY YEARS ON BACK COUNTRY SURVIVAL

This book has been written for the purpose of educating the public, young and old alike, about how to use common sense survival skills when traveling the wilderness areas and back country of the Northwest.

I was born in 1915 on the Flathead Reservation in northwestern Montana, and grew up among the Salish Indians. I have been a rancher and professional packer, guide and outfitter for over 56 years.

Every year we read or hear about people losing or nearly losing their lives while in the back country and, sadly, the loss of life is often due to lack of wilderness survival knowledge. I hope this book will be of some value to people who live the outdoors, whether enjoying recreational activities, hunting or working.

Planning A Trip Or Outing In Advance

Ask yourself the following questions before leaving on a trip.
a. Where am I going?
b. How long will I be gone?
c. What is my starting point and point of return?
d. Have I given someone adequate information about my plans and trip in case of trouble?
e. What is my means of travel (foot, horseback, boat, etc.)?
f. What do I need to take?
1. Proper clothing, gloves
2. Matches and cigarette lighter
3. A fair sized candle
4. A good hatchet
5. A good knife and whetstone

From this point-of-view high on a mountainside, one gets an overwhelming perspective of what's really at play when hiking in remote wilderness country. Many people not used to mountain travel have been deceived when looking down at scenes like this of the two meadows in the center of this picture. They've gotten the feeling that it wasn't very far down to them, but they're actually about 12 miles away. To get to those meadows, the hiker would have to cover some very rough country, cross two streams, traverse several deep and steep ravines, and travel through dense, heavy timber. This is the stuff of which wilderness survival problems are made.

    6. Rope and canteen
    7. String and extra shoestring
    8. Small first aid kit
    9. Needle and thread
  10. Compass and map
  11. Insect repellant
  12. Copper or other wire

Know The Terrain You Are Traveling In
Before you set out on your trip, get a map of the area that you will be using and study each trail, the direction it goes, and where each trail leads. Study the streams, the direction of main flow, and where they go. We know that the little streams will lead to larger streams, and that the larger streams will lead to a main water course, usually a river. Remember that most of the main ridges on a mountain will run in the same general direction as the streams. Try to determine the distance between points, but don't forget that a mile in the mountains can seem a lot longer than a mile on flat land. I have been fortunate because I have never been lost in the woods, although there have been many times that I didn't know for sure where I was. It never bothers me much, because I know that if I don't get out today, I will get out tomorrow or the next day, as long as I use common sense.

Proper Clothing
When I travel into the back country or into the woods, I go so I can enjoy my outing. I would never go into the mountains or timber country any distance without being fully clothed. This means full length pants, a long sleeved shirt, good walking shoes and socks. If all I had to wear was shorts, a short sleeved shirt and no head cover, I would refuse to go at all. Your body needs to be protected in every way, and though shorts may give you a little more freedom in walking, protection is more important.

You may plan on staying on the mapped trails, but there are many things you may encounter that could cause you to leave the trail, so be prepared for anything. Keep in mind that in the summer you may get into a lot of mosquitoes or other insects.

Remember, your feet are one of the main parts of your body, so take care of them. Be sure that your shoes fit properly before you leave your home. I have never had a blister since I was a small boy, because when I buy shoes, I get them large enough to wear with two pair of socks. I always wear two, and sometimes even three pairs of socks when I am outside all day, or climbing in the hills. If you begin to feel a hot spot or a sore spot while

This is my type of boot. Note the knobby sole and heel with a sharp, square edge — and the eight-inch top.

These are the two pairs of boots the author uses most when traveling in the back country. Not only do they have the types of soles that give good, safe footing under most field conditions but they also hold up well under heavy use — an essential consideration because once you're in the back country, you can't replace your footwear.

hiking, don't let it go. Stop right away or you will soon have a blister or raw spot. If you don't have protective Band-Aids you can usually help cushion the spot by pulling your sock down a ways and doubling it over the sore spot. Do all that you can to keep your shoes and feet dry; never wade through water or streams if you can find another way across. If you have no other way, remove your socks and wade across wearing only your shoes. If the water is deep, take off your pants and any other necessary clothes so they don't get wet either. You always want to have warm, dry clothes to wear. I have seen many people wade across streams fully clothed who regretted their foolishness later. Always try to use good common sense while out-of-doors. I wear leather boots when it is dry, and rubber boots when it is damp and

This view of a group and saddle horses and pack mules on top of the Chinese Wall in the Bob Marshall Wilderness gives an excellent example of just how vast the wilderness really is. This is the sort of remote, rough country in which both the foot and horseback traveler must be considerate of many safety factors so that survival doesn't become an issue.

raining.

When you are planning to go into mountain areas, buy a good quality shoe or boot. The sole should be a Vibram or another non-slip sole with a heel of some kind. Plain leather soles are not good as they get very slick on steep ground. A good sole will enable your feet to stay firmly where you step. If you are slipping and sliding, you will soon be tired and worn out, and may not be able to make it to your destination. Avoid cowboy boots; they are only good for horseback riding. In selecting your rubber boots, avoid a sole with a rounded edge, especially for use in snow and on sidehills or steep ground because they slip and you will have trouble keeping your footing. Find a boot with a square-edged sole

The small daybag at the right comfortably holds everything the author needs to cover a warm weather survival situation, including a raincoat, a blanket, a compass, knife sharpeners, string, leather thong, drinking cup, a candle, wire, and a role of plastic tarp for an emergency covering.

— that is where the sole comes to an abrupt right angle. Knobby type soles are very good, or soles with a deep cut design. I always encourage all of my hunters, or any winter climbers that I am with, to have good non-slip footwear, and have found that if they don't, they are usually not able to keep up with the guide or their group.

Higher boots also protect your ankles from scrapes, punctures and bruises, and support the ankles from strain as well. The lower your boots or shoes are, the more likely you are to get pebbles, twigs, or snow stuck in the sides. I usually wear a rubber boot that is about 12 inches high, and an eight inch high leather boot.

I never tuck my pant legs inside my socks, or boots —

This is the famous Chinese Wall in the Bob Marshall Wilderness in Montana. It is approximately 15 miles long and 1,000 feet of vertical cliff. From this point, you would need to travel seven or eight miles in either direction to get around the end of the wall. When traveling in the back country by either foot or horseback, you may encounter hazardous terrain such as this and need to plan your route carefully.

especially in snowy or rainy weather — for the simple reason that the moisture that gets on your clothing will run down your pant leg and into your boots, and soon you will have wet feet. Putting your pant leg over the boot will allow the water to go over the boot and help keep your feet dry. Don't put your pant legs down too low over your boots, or they will be more apt to catch sticks in the edge of the cuffs and trip you. This is why all the older loggers "stagged" or cut off of their britches and wore suspenders. When the snow is deep enough to work up under my pant legs, I take some twine or string out of my hip pocket and take a couple of wraps around each leg, tying the pants down. Be sure to leave enough slack in the pant leg so that your knees can work and bend

Here the author is describing to a wilderness hiker the best way for her to get to a point she wants to see — and in the process doing something he always recommends, making a small drawing or map of how to get to, or back from, a specific destination.

freely.

In general, I am referring to backcountry travel in the northwestern states, Canada and Alaska, and what clothing is proper for this type of terrain. There are a lot of good trails and parks in these parts of the country, but outside of the parks the good trails usually don't go very far. If I were not real familiar with the area that I was going into, I would never leave my car on the road if I was going any distance without wearing what I call "long clothes." Long clothes consist of a shirt with sleeves and full length pants. In the Northwest some of the things you may encounter along the trails or hiking cross-country are plants such as poison oak, poison ivy and stinging nettles. There are briars of many kinds, including rose bushes, hawthorne, blackberry and raspberry bushes, thistle and devil's club. Besides that, there are brush thickets you may have to push your way through, plus sharp

Once the weather gets colder, these wool liners and leather mittens, plus the wool stocking hat, go into the author's daybag. They cover most short-term, emergency situations by providing protection for two basic cold weather survival needs — your head and hands.

sticks and rocks, and pitchy logs to avoid. Common insects found in these wilderness areas are mosquitoes, horseflies, deer flies, ticks, and many kinds of spiders and bees. There are some poisonous snakes. I would not like to run through the brush or climb a tree to get way from a bear or some other animal with bare legs and arms. Your long clothes will protect your skin from being scratched and punctured, and from sunburn, which can be very bad. The pant legs may save you from a snake or animal bite, and will protect you from many insect bites. In the hot sun, your clothes will keep you cooler than if the sun shines on your bare skin.

If I am going out overnight or longer, I always take some kind of head cover. Above all, don't forget your raincoat, as the weather in the Northern Rockies can vary day to day from 90 degrees plus to sub-zero temperatures. A cold rain, or even snow, can come in quickly in June, July, or August, so be prepared for any kind of weather. And don't forget your gloves. Not only will they protect you from briars, poisonous plants, and insects, but they will protect against the cold as well.

THE SIGNIFICANCE OF A HATCHET

Your knife and hatchet are the most important tools that you can carry but both of them should be good and sharp. But if not being used properly they can be very dangerous.

You always want to cut away from any of your body parts. When making shavings or sharpening a peg or stake, it is best to put the end of the peg or stake onto a log for a solid support to cut or chop onto. When chopping with a hatchet or an axe, especially a short handled axe, and you don't have a log or wood of some kind for the axe to go into, and you should happen to miss your target, the hatchet or axe has a very good chance of cutting into your legs or any part of your body.

While chopping, be especially careful that there are no limbs or anything of any kind for the axe or hatchet to catch onto. Always look above your head for limbs or anything else on which they could get caught. If the axe catches on or hits any object, the axe may be deflected and may go anyplace or direction and it may cut into you. I have several scars on my own body from this happening to me so be very careful when chopping or cutting.

Important Items To Take

Once you have studied the map and decided where to go, you need to figure out what to take with you. Along with good clothes, be sure you have a map and compass, and good matches in a watertight container. A cigarette lighter and a candle may be handy. I never go into the woods or mountains without a hatchet. If I were blindfolded and taken a long ways back in a wilderness area that was unknown to me, to be turned loose to survive on my own, and I was given the opportunity to have one tool, I would pick my hatchet above any other tool, even a gun or a knife. I know that I can survive for quite a while with my hatchet, and I can at least build a shelter and bed, so I can be halfway warm. I firmly believe that every person going into the backcountry should carry a hatchet, learn how to use it, what to use it for, and how to keep it sharp.

There are a lot of different hatchets and hunting knives on the market, but a large share of them aren't worth carrying on your belt. However, there are a few good ones available if you look for them. I carry a 1 1/2 lb. True Temper Hatchet with a wooden handle. You need to know how to keep a handle tight in the head, because in dry weather the wood may shrink a little and loosen in the head. Also, you should know how to put a new

This is my belt knife, hatchet, rope and canteen.

handle in it properly, in case you should break the original. I have replaced mine two or three times in the last 30 years. There are hatchets with steel and rubber handles that are good, just be sure to get an axe or hatchet of good quality that weighs one to two pounds. Make sure the steel of both your knife and hatchet is a type that can be sharpened and will hold an edge. Most sporting good stores carry a lot of different types of hunting knives, but few are made with good steel that will hold a cutting edge. My sons, our hunting guides, and I all buy our knives from butcher supply houses, as their knives are designed for professional meat cutters, and you can be sure of getting a good knife. We make our own sheaths for our knives and hatchets, but you can have someone else make them to your liking at most leather shops if you don't want to make your own.

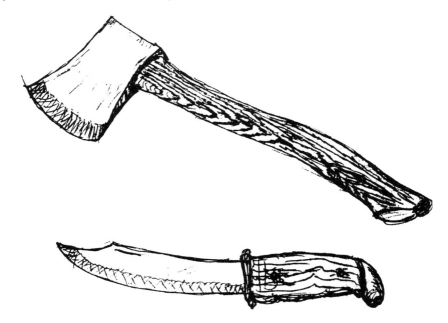

I like this type of knife and hatchet.

SHARPENING YOUR AXE AND KNIFE

I always try to keep my axes and knives sharp enough to cut my whiskers, and a new knife or hatchet is never sharp enough to suit me, so I resharpen the new tools I buy. There are several new sharpening devices on the market, but I still prefer the old method. My sharpening tools are an eight inch file, a steel, and a good stone with a fine and coarse side. It is very important to keep a long taper on your axe or knife all the years that you use it. The taper is where the blade starts to thin down toward the cutting edge. If you don't grind all the way up on the taper the blade will start to get blunt after several sharpenings, and a tool isn't much good to you if it doesn't cut well.

First, I like to start sharpening with my file, starting at the top part of the taper on the blade, and take off the same amount from both sides, while gradually working outward to the cutting edge of the blade. Then I take the coarse side of the stone and start to grind in a circular motion, starting at the upper part again and gradually working outward to the cutting edge. You can apply a little pressure if you want, and it will cut a little faster. Slack off on the pressure when you get close to the cutting edge. Now take the fine side of the stone and repeat the process, again starting at the upper part and working outward.

It's on the finishing part that you need to be careful and have a good eye and good feel. For the finishing touches I use the smooth side of the stone, grinding in a circular motion, and starting at the far tip of the blade. Still using the circular motion, move toward the handle. This procedure causes the little cutting edges that are too small to see with the naked eye to point back toward the handle of the knife. This in turn causes the knife to cut better when being pulled through something. It's best to keep the stone surface as flat as possible, so always try to use the full surface an equal amount.

When you are putting the last of the finishing touches on your axe or knife, turn the blade up so the sharp edge is toward the sky and look closely along the cutting edge for shiny spots. You may have to turn the blade a little one way or the other, holding it toward the light. If there are shiny spots, it's not sharp in those spots yet, so you will have to grind some more, especially on the shiny areas. Another way to check the blade is to run your hand over the cutting edge. If the skin on your thumb kind of slides over the edge, it's not sharp yet, but if you experience a slight pulling feeling, the blade will probably cut you quite easily.

If you are very careful while working the blade edge over the stone on the finishing touches, you will be able to feel a slight pull where the blade is pulling into the stone and getting sharper. Don't put any pressure on the stone or you will be bending the finish edge over. Instead, go lightly from one side to the other.

You also want to keep your eyes on the stone and the very edge of the blade. As you work, you should see a little bit of stone dust start to gather on the blade edge. The dust should gather the full length of the blade, indicating that it is sharp the full length. Be sure to work both sides of your blade an equal amount of time. It takes a little practice to learn to do a perfect job on these tools.

Take your steel and give your knife a few strokes, and your blade is ready for use. You want to hold the steel pointed away from you in your left hand, and with the right pull the knife blade across the steel with the cutting edge facing you. Be careful not to cut yourself. Pull your blade full length from one side to the other and take a few strokes, making sure that the cutting edge is touching the steel.

After you use the knife for a while, and you feel it is not cutting as well as it should, give it a few more strokes, using the same number of strokes on each side. Don't use too much pressure; remember, all you want the steel to do is to straighten up the little cutting edges that are too small for the naked eye to see. If you use an uneven number of strokes on each side of the steel, you may be turning the cutting edge too much one direction. Your hatchet is your most important tool in the backcountry, so know how to use and care for it. If you are ever in an emergency situation, it may save your life.

FIRE BUILDING

My old body has been warmed by wood fires for 80 years. I have built thousands of fires, for camp fires and for different types of wood stoves, and I have cleared many acres of land and burned the timber slash. Today, the majority of people don't have much experience with camp fires, and generally do not know how to build a fire properly and keep it going without a lot of effort.

Nearly everyone that I have known, except people that I trained myself, has been taught to build the popular tepee (tripod shaped) fire, or else they want to crisscross their wood in every direction. While the American Indians lived in and cooked in and heated their lodges, they did not use a tepee fire because it is almost impossible to cook on. And because this type of fire consumes fuel quickly, it takes at least one person working steadily to try to keep it burning. If the wood isn't good and dry the fire will soon go out.

I stress never putting even one piece of wood crossway into the fire, because in order for a fire to burn well, the wood has to constantly be getting into the hot part of the fire. In a tepee fire the sticks at the top will often bind each other and keep the wood from coming down into the fire, and if it does come down each piece will lay in a different direction. One piece may not burn as quickly as the others, and every piece that falls on that one may be held off the fire, and so on, until eventually your fire goes out. So remember, if you put a stick crossway or tepee style, you are hurting your fire.

A few years ago, I had a large group of Explorer Scouts back in the Mission Mountain Wilderness area. One young man who was watching me as I got ready to start building my fire said, "You were born with the Indians and you don't know how to build a fire yet? Let me show you how to build one."

I thought, well, we are never too old to learn something new, so I let him build a fire for me. After awhile he finally got his tepee fire going. It burned quite well for a few minutes, then went out, and he couldn't get it going again without starting a new one. His fire was of the same type that I had first tried to build as a boy, and is the same type that most people build. After his lesson, I went ahead and built my own fire.

Before you build a fire you need to be sure that it will be in a safe place where it will not have a chance to spread and possibly start a forest fire. Be extra careful in dry weather. If you are at a spot where there have been other fires built, and it is safe, use the same spot. Be sure you are on bare ground and don't build the fire on any dry vegetation, or over shallow growing tree roots. The fire will damage the roots, which will in turn cause damage

Getting wood ready for a fire directly in front of my shelter.

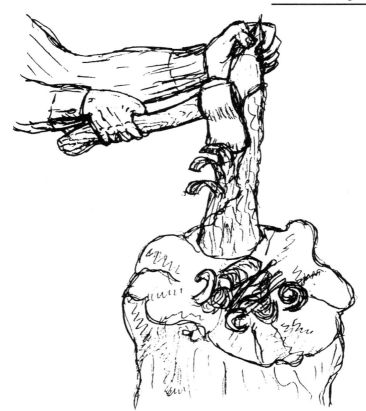

Making shavings with my hatchet from a dry chunk of wood by setting it up right on top of a stump.

to the trees. A fire can burn underground a long distance and can continue to burn for several days, so choose your spot carefully.

The main thing to know about starting a fire is to know your wood. That is, which wood will start easily, burn the best, and hold the fire the longest. There is no point in building a fire larger than is needed; it's foolish to waste wood. First determine how large a fire you need, for instance, whether it is only to cook on, or whether you want it to last all night. For an all-night fire I select two large pieces of wood or logs that I can carry, preferably something that will not burn very well or quickly, so it can even be damp or wet. For a smaller fire, use two smaller pieces.

One of the best sources of fire-starting material when in the woods is a scar on a tree trunk, often caused by lightning or some other abrasion, where pitchy material accumulates as the tree tries to heal itself. Small pieces of this can be cut away with your hatchet, or broken off, to be used as a good fire starter.

Determine how wide you want your fire and place your two logs parallel to each other as far apart as you want the fire to be in width. A space about two feet wide would be wide enough for a larger fire. If one log is smaller than the other, use the smaller one on the side that you will be working from. Gather all your wood before starting the fire. The two logs will keep your fire in place and prevent a breeze or wind from blowing under your fire and blowing smoke all over. Also, the logs will act as a self-feeder for the fire, and your other wood won't roll off the fire, but will remain contained between the two outside logs.

Next, gather all the wood that you will feed the fire with (it can be of any size or shape), and put it within reach of the fire spot. When gathering the wood for starter, remember that all trees, even green trees, have a certain amount of dead twigs or moss on them, and usually some dead needles on the underside of the

Shavings made from pieces of pitchy wood. These were made with my knife and will be used for starting the fire.

Another good fire-starting technique is to shave off large chips from a piece of pitchy wood, using either your hatchet or a knife, and place the chips right on the fire bed and light with a match.

branches. Gather a good armload of these and keep the finer, smaller pieces apart from the coarser ones. Usually, this tinder will work well, except in extremely damp weather. Gather a handful of the finest bits of moss, twigs or needles and try to keep the pieces parallel to each other. If you are going to use a match, it may be wise to have a little dry rock on which to strike the match. Put the rock close to where you want to start the fire so you don't have to move the match more than a few inches to the fuel, otherwise, if there is a breeze it may go out. Take a dry match from your container and check for a breeze. If there is one, build your fire so that the breeze will blow the fire into the fuel. I suggest carrying wooden matches. Strike a match and keep it in a downward angle with your hand cupped around it so it doesn't go out. With your other hand hold your kindling just off the ground, placing your match on the underside so that the fire wants to come upward. As the fire grows lay your kindling down gently on it, and as it progresses keep adding kindling. Don't get in too big of a hurry, but keep adding slightly larger pieces as it grows.

If you can't get the fire to burn, you need to find some pitch. Remember that you shouldn't be out there without a good knife and your faithful hatchet, which should weigh about one pound or more and be of good quality. Be sure you have them both good and sharp before you leave home. Take your hatchet and look for a dead standing tree, or a green tree with an old scar where a chunk of bark may have been knocked off in previous years. A damaged tree usually causes a surplus of sap to gather and harden in the wound area. Pine trees are more apt to have pitchy wood than others, and sometimes the roots from a fallen or uprooted tree will have it. Occasionally, you can find pitch in the core of an old rotten fir tree that has fallen. This is the best type of pitch because it will burn like gasoline.

The pitchy wood is always hard or solid with a brown tinge in color. It will have a strong pitchy smell, and water cannot penetrate the wood well. If you cannot find any pitch, take your hatchet, chop into the side of a dry standing pine tree and take out a chunk of wood. If there are no pine, the next best kind would be

An essential element of good fire building is that you gather good, dry wood. Often, as is the case with this old Douglas Fir, the dead lower branches make very good firewood.

spruce, and after that, fir, or any other dead tree. Gather up the chips and chunks of pitch and take them to your fire spot. Place them on one of the big logs you first brought to your fire spot and chop them into fine pieces. The log will provide a solid base and make it easier to chop your kindling, while at the same time protecting the hatchet blade from being nicked or from becoming dull. Remember, you may need that hatchet tomorrow or the next day, so keep it sharp by avoiding cutting into the ground or onto rocks or metal.

Once you have the kindling ready, take out your good old-faithful knife, and taking one piece of kindling at a time, put one end down on your log, so that you are holding the piece of wood vertically, but at an angle. To make shavings, start your knife at the upper part of your kindling and cut thin slices off the sides. Slice enough shavings so that you have at least a good handful,

The author with an armload of dead tree branches taken within an arm's reach of the ground and then carried back to the campsite. Utilizing these branches gives you a variety of wood size, too.

then shave a few more, this time leaving the slivers attached to the lower part of your kindling. Pick up a handful of shavings, keeping each piece parallel with the other, with the tapered or flared end pointing outward, and hold it in position where you're going to start the fire. Light the flared end from the underside, then lay your burning handful of shavings down gently.

Start feeding your fire, first using the loose shavings. It is important that you place each shaving parallel to the others. Start laying your pieces of kindling with the shaved ends in the same way, parallel to each other. Then follow with smaller pieces of wood. Be very sure that you do not put even one piece of wood on crossway, or you will ruin the fire. Once the fire is going you can use greener or wetter wood, and it will still burn. This type of fire will burn evenly and won't go out until all of the wood is gone. The wood won't roll off the fire because you have placed it in a parallel position. Common sense will tell you that this fire will feed itself. As the fire burns, each piece of wood will automatically roll one by one onto the hottest part of the fire, because there is no where else for it to go.

Use the same method of fire building for a small camp or cooking fire, a wood heater stove, fireplace or wood range, or for burning a slash pile. When starting a fire in a stove or fireplace, build your fire as close to the draft intake as possible, and when refueling a stove, pull the hot coals and fire close to the draft before putting more wood in, and place the wood on top of the coals. The draft will blow the fire into the wood and cause it to burn well.

It seems to be a natural instinct for most people to want to put their wood crossway or angling across the fire. If you are one of those people, try to break yourself of the habit, it only hinders

Preparation of a fire bed includes the staking of two small logs laid parallel to each other. This will both contain the fire and allow you to feed more wood onto it, as required.

your fire. I've watched a lot of people try to get a fire going in their stoves. When they have trouble most of them lay the blame on the quality of the wood, but usually when I have gone to help them, I've found that the stove is full of wood piled crisscross. The wood can't possibly come down on the fire, and consequently, it is impossible for it to burn. Sometimes the problem is that people have started the fire in the middle of the stove instead of by the draft intake.

When you're in the woods it's always wise to carry a little piece of pitch wood in your pack or pocket, as the following anecdote illustrates. My granddaughter was getting ready to leave on a spring backpack trip with three other women, so her father cut a small batch of pitch shavings for her to carry along in her backpack to use as fire starter. The weather worsened as they climbed, and they were caught in a slush storm just before sunset

The author recommends that all wood inside the fire pit run in the same direction to facilitate proper burning. The starter kindling at left will be laid lengthwise in the fire pit when the fire is lit.

A warm, contained fire like the one in front of this temporary shelter will provide plenty of warmth. Note the placement of the firewood where it can be easily grabbed when it's time to replenish the fire.

as they reached Terrace Lake. The clouds rolled in and rain and snow came down so heavily that it was pitch black by the time they reached the lake shore. The slush was knee deep everywhere and they couldn't find a bit of dry kindling, even with a flashlight. They could hear branches snapping and rocks bouncing by from little mud slides that were coming down the slopes all around them in the darkness.

While my granddaughter and one woman struggled to get the tents up, the other two women tried to get a fire going. Every time they would get a little flame started, the slushy rain would drown it in a new torrent. Everyone was soaked, even under their rain gear and my granddaughter's wasn't very adequate, as she sheepishly admitted later. One woman seemed to be in the beginning stages of hypothermia. When she realized they couldn't start the fire, my granddaughter dug out the pitch, which she had kept wrapped in a plastic bag, and they had a good fire going in no time. They got themselves and the suffering woman warmed up, and made a hot meal. Their extra clothes and sleeping bags were pretty dry because they had lined their packs with plastic garbage bags, so they managed to pass the night without being too cold and miserable. They all felt very kindly toward my son for his foresight as they trudged home the next day.

Matches

Before you go to the woods to camp, or for any reason, be sure not to forget your matches, and check to make sure they are good quality and will light easily. I feel that wooden matches are better to carry than paper matches, but you'll still want to check out a few from any batch you select to carry with you because some brands don't light as well as others. I carry a watertight match container full of matches, plus I roll a few matches in two separate bunches, put them in wax paper or little plastic bags, and wrap a rubber band around each bunch. The rubber band will hold them packed tightly so that they won't rub together and ignite in your pocket. I put each package in an inside pocket to keep them from getting damp. It's also a good idea to carry a cigarette lighter, but don't rely on it alone, because it may fail you and not light. Always carry some matches also. Sometimes a fair sized, short candle can be helpful in starting your fire. There are also some good commercially made fire starters available on the market.

FAMILIARIZE YOURSELF WITH YOUR CAMP AREA

There are many different types of camp gear, and many different ideas on how a camp should be set up. Everyone has their own way of setting up camp, including myself, and though I wouldn't attempt to try to tell someone how to build their camp, I would like to offer some pointers on familiarizing yourself with your camp area.

If you are camping in an area that you are not familiar with and you plan to leave your camp temporarily to hunt or hike, or whatever, first take out your compass and map and pinpoint where your camp is located on the map. Then look around in all directions and memorize all the better landmarks. Usually the highest peaks or hills make the best landmarks, but a rock ledge or deep canyon might also work. Each rock or hill is a little different, so try to record in your mind what each landmark looks like. Next set your compass with the pointer to the north and check the direction of each of your main landmarks from your camp. If you are by a stream, remember which side of the stream your camp is on, which direction the water is flowing, and how much water is in the stream bed. But don't forget that the amount of water that flows in a stream in a mountain area can vary. A stream can go underground and then reappear, especially at the base of a mountain.

Before leaving camp check to make sure that the fire is completely out. In deciding what to take with you, first be sure to have the right type of clothing. If it is cloudy and there is a chance of rain or snow, bring your raincoat. If the weather should get bad it is also nice to have your rain pants.

Whenever he goes into the woods, the author carries these items — a canteen, rope, hatchet and knife — on an extra belt. He also recommends that you carry gloves with you on every trip to protect your hands when rough work is required.

I always carry certain items in my pockets that might come in handy, including a good supply of toilet paper, matches in waterproof containers in three different pockets, and if I am hunting, a few sheets of paper toweling. Check your matches to make sure they are dry and will light. I also carry a small whetstone, a compass, a pocket knife, extra leather shoestring, several feet of light cord, and a piece of copper wire about three feet long.

This wire is handy for a lot of different things. I've used it to temporarily sew up torn clothing, and I've sewn lots of shoes together when the soles have pulled off. I saw one fellow a year and a half after I had sewn his soles on his shoes back in the mountains, and he was still wearing the same pair of shoes! You can use the wire to clean a gun barrel by fastening a rag to one end of a piece of wire, and then pushing the wire through the barrel far enough to get a hold of it and pull the rag through.

I wear an extra belt with my hatchet, hunting knife, canteen, and about 15 feet of rope. I put my lunch in the back of my shirt. It's wise to carry extra candy bars, or prunes or raisins. You may prefer to carry some or all of these items in a little pack, along with a first aid kit if you want.

Be sure you know which direction you are going from your camp, and after you have gone a little distance, look back at your campsite and try to memorize what it looks like. For instance, are the trees tall or short, thick or thin, are there hills or anything else to remember? It's always good to look back at your camp because it will appear different when you are coming in from another direction.

As you go along, be alert for anything that might be a marker for you, such as a peak, a hill, a long ridge, tall trees, a burnt snag, cliffs or ledges, a big boulder, or streams. Keep thinking back to where these markers are.

LOST IN THE WOODS

If you should get lost, or if you are just a long way from camp and it's near nightfall, don't try to travel in the dark unless you are sure you can get to your destination. It can be very dangerous traveling in the dark. It's possible to puncture an eye on a protruding branch or to trip over logs, and even to walk over a cliff or fall into a deep hole. There are so many ways a person can get hurt that I think it's best to camp out for the night, especially in heavy timber. If you are on a good trail you may do quite well by feeling along with your feet.

I think the thing that most people fear the most about getting lost in the woods is being alone in the dark with all the wild animals. Well, since there are just as many animals out there in the daytime as there are at night, they would be the least of my worries. What you should be most concerned about is over-exertion, over-exposure to the elements and hypothermia. A big share of people who get lost panic and start running and yelling through the woods. My boys and I have found several lost people, and most of them were people who had panicked and lost their ability to reason.

It's easy for anyone to get turned around in a snowstorm, or in fog, in which case a compass can come in handy. If I don't have a compass with me and I want to get through a large area of thick woods without ending up going in circles, I pick out an object or a tree and walk to it in as straight a line as possible, and then pick out another marker pointing in the same direction before reaching the first one. I keep on in this manner and usually I will come out right where I want to, or very close.

If you get turned around and need to get a secure sense of direction to get out of a place, remember that small streams like the one in this piece of rugged country always lead to a larger stream — which, in turn, will lead to a river and lower elevations.

If you do get turned around or lost, don't allow yourself to panic. It's not that bad to have to stay over night in the woods. If it is dry weather you may not need a fire, but if it is wet and cold you should plan on building one. Remember, the most important thing you need to do if you have to stay overnight in the woods is to keep your body dry. If you are starting to shiver, you had better get yourself a fire built and a shelter set up right away, or you may become too cold and disoriented to perform even simple tasks as hypothermia sets in.

If you have a feeling that you may not be able to find your way out of the area you are traveling in, start watching for a good piece of pitch wood as you go along. Sometimes you can get it from the roots of an uprooted tree, or in the center of a big, old fire log that has rotted, or from the dead top of a pine tree. Or, as

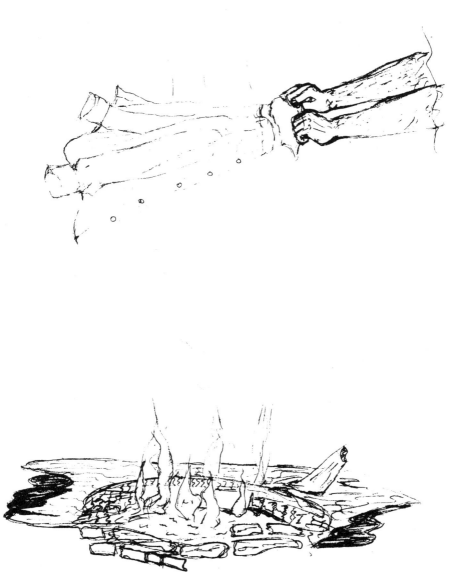

Dry out the boughs in the same way as drying your clothing, by swinging them back and forth over the fire. This will dry them more quickly than any other way.

I mentioned before, look for trees with an old scar and cut a piece out with your hatchet. When you find a good piece, put it in your pocket to use to start your fire later. Give yourself plenty of time to fix a camp before it gets dark, and before you get too tired. Try to keep your body dry, and don't exert yourself to the point of sweating. If you have your rain clothes with you, and you haven't been sweating, you should be dry.

It's always a few degrees warmer under a big bushy tree, or in a thicket of trees. If you find a good, bushy tree, it may be a good place to stop. Check around the base, because, quite often a bushy tree will have a thick mat of dry needles under it. If they are wet on top, dig down through them; sometimes they are dry underneath. If they are, you may have found a good place to spend the night.

I have buried myself like a bear in needles to keep warm. Most people don't realize how much heat a person can get, or save, from just plain green boughs of fir, spruce, cedar, or even pine. The only drawback with spruce and pine is that they have very sharp points. Juniper, which is often mistaken for cedar, is also sharp. There are many ways boughs can be used for protection from the cold.

One of the best ways I have found to make a bed to keep from getting too cold is to find two logs, or pieces of logs a little bit larger around than your body and a little longer than you are high. If you can't find any that large, use smaller ones; when put in place they can be blocked up higher. Try to find a fairly level place for your bed, on the side which is protected from the wind as you will get less rain and snow blown in on the sheltered side. Lay the two logs parallel to each other, just a bit wider than your body.

If you are with another person, make it wide enough for both of you. If you have dry needles available, pile them two or three inches thick in the bottom of your bed. If you can find it, dry, rotten, crumbly wood will work in place of needles. If there are any cracks or holes under your logs, plug them so that no draft can come in. Next, put a layer of dry boughs over the dead

ABOUT 4 FOOT LONG
DIGGING TOOL

needles, placing them so they are all in the same direction. Poke all the stem parts toward the entrance and down to the ground. This way they won't poke you when you lay down in your bed. You will need a couple of armloads.

If the boughs are wet or have snow on them, first shake them dry as best you can, then bring them over to your fire. Take a few at a time and swing them back and forth over the fire. They will dry very quickly and you need to be careful because they ignite easily.

Now that you have the bottom of your bed done, take the larger boughs that you have gathered and break them to fit across the width between the two logs. Keep putting them on from log to log until you have the bed covered. Use the larger limbs first to give the top more support. If you want to build the bed large enough for two people, or if it should rain, you may want to cut about four poles just long enough to fit crossway over your two logs, spacing them equally apart. Then cut one more pole the same length as your bed is long, and lay it lengthwise across the four short poles down the middle. This will give better support, and also a little pitch to the top. Most boughs have a little bend in them, so lay them with the bend up, and with the small end to the outside. They will shed more water that way. Lay them all crossway of the bed.

Be sure you don't build the bed too high or too wide. Leave only enough room so that you can crawl into it without

In looking over a large portion of varying terrain, like this scene in the Bob Marshall Wilderness, remember that what you're looking at is only a small part of the countryside. It helps for you to pick out major landmarks so you can always keep your bearings as you move around.

disturbing it. Most people try to make their shelter too big, but the bigger you build it the colder it will be, and the more materials it will take to build it. Once you have the boughs in place, see if you can find some old pieces of bark. Sometimes you can knock some off the old logs. If you find some, lay the pieces on in a fashion to drain the rain off of your bed. Put the rounded part down so it will catch the water or snow and let it run off like in a trough. Or, lay two pieces, rounded side down, spacing them apart a little. Place a third piece of bark on top of the first two, except with the rounded part up, so that you cover the space between the first two pieces. Keep doing this until the shelter is completely covered.

Usually there is a lot of vegetation in the woods. Dig up anything you can find such as small plants, roots and all, dirt, grass, rotten wood, leaves. To make a good digging tool, take your hatchet and try to find a little pole or stout limb that has a branch on it that would make a hook. Cut it so that the handle part is about four feet long, and the hook part about six inches long. Cut the hook part at an angle so that it will dig better. With this tool you can do a lot of digging in a hurry. Put everything you dig up on top of your bed, and try to make it as air tight as possible, except for the entrance. Cut enough extra boughs so that after you get inside you can cover the entrance, which should be just large enough so that you can get in and be able to turn over. When you go to bed, don't take any of your clothes off, not even your cap, raincoat, or shoes.

You may not be comfortable when you have to stay out in the woods, but you can survive. One note of caution: if you decide to build a fire be careful not to start it in the needles, or you may not be able to get it out. Please note that these instructions are for life and death situations, and I don't encourage people in the backcountry to disturb the natural environment and cut live vegetation indiscriminately. It may be best not to cut down any green trees unless they are growing so thickly together that they can't grow well. A few branches or boughs cut from the lower part of a bushy tree is not harmful and can be beneficial to the tree.

BUILDING A SHELTER

Nowadays you can buy real light, tough plastic that can be rolled up into a small, pliable bundle and carried in a pack. Get a piece four to five feet wide by seven to eight feet long. You can wrap it around you or use it over your bed or shelter. If you have cord of some kind, you can tie a little rock in each corner of the plastic as a weight to keep it in place, and if it is windy, lay a few branches over it to hold it down.

You can make an easy shelter in just a few minutes with your piece of plastic by cutting seven poles for the frame. You don't have to be choosy — try to find dead wood — anything you can find that's not too rotten. Cut two poles about five feet long for the front part of the A frame, four poles about six or seven feet long, and one pole about seven to eight feet long. Tie the small ends of the two shorter poles together on the small ends to make an A-frame. Lay the seven foot pole out on the ground with the big end by the A-frame poles. Stand the A-frame up and pick up the seven foot pole by the butt, leaving the small end on the ground. Tie the butt end to the top of the A-frame, tilting the A-frame back just a little to enable it to stand by itself. Leaving the A-frame open for the doorway, tie the six to seven foot poles to the frame parallel to the ground by placing two poles on each side, and spacing them an equal distance from the ground to the peak. Then cover the shelter with your plastic tarp, or whatever you have available. (See illustration.)

Sometimes you can find two logs or fallen trees that are lying about six feet apart and get in between the logs. The larger the logs the better. If there is snow on the ground clean a spot off to the bare ground. One of the logs will make a simple base to build a lean-to. Take your hatchet and cut at least three poles, making them long enough so that you can put the butt end on the ground. Then angle them over the top of the log with the small end sticking out about four or five feet past the base log, pointing toward the other log. Space the poles equally with the outside ones about as far apart as you are tall, approximately six feet.

If the ground isn't frozen, you may want to sharpen the butt ends and shove them into the ground a little. If the ground is too hard, you can lay a log or something heavy on the butt ends to keep the poles from tipping up when you cover the lean-to. Cut another pole about six feet long. Take two pieces of cord, rope, or wire that you have carried with you, and tie the end of the last pole to the two outside poles right out onto the end to hold the poles in place. You may want to put one or two more poles on. You need not tie these as the boughs for the roof will hold them in place. Again, if you can find old pieces of bark, use that to help

A half-finished shelter. Note that the two upright poles are tilted back a little for stability. Any kind of poles can be used.

cover the lean-to. Put the boughs on with the stems pointing uphill. Be sure to start your cover from the bottom up, with each bough overlapping the one below, so that they will shed rain, just like shingles.

Build your fire directly across from your lean-to, right against the other big log. This log will help your fire continue to burn. If you want a fire all night it will take a good pile of wood, so bring in anything you can find, from small pieces to as big as you can carry. The wood doesn't all have to be dry; it will burn as it dries out in the fire. The big log will reflect a lot of the heat toward your lean-to, and the top of the lean-to should reflect a little of the heat back down.

Once you have your camp set up you can fix a place to sit or lie down. Although you can rest while sitting, it is a lot better to be able to lie down at least part of the night. Bark or dry needles make good insulation, if you can find some to use for your

A complete shelter looking from the back end. This shelter is only about three feet high in the front.

bed. If you want you can cover the bark with boughs. If you are going to be lying against the log, it may be wise to put a few boughs against it to help keep you warm. Block off the ends of the lean-to, and cover them with boughs or bark. You can hold in body heat by covering up with dry boughs.

If you can't find a place with two big logs, you may have to settle for only one log for the lean-to. Build your fire in front of the lean-to. If you can only find smaller logs, you can build them up and make a lean-to over the frame. Another simple way to build a shelter is to find three or more little trees about five or six feet high, and growing close together. Take two of the little trees and bend them over each other, tie them together with some rope or string. Pull a third tree down over the tied ones and tie it down over them. Cover the frame with sticks, boughs, bark, etc., leaving one of the spaces between the trees open for a door. Then gather boughs to make a nest for yourself inside, taking care to

This is an easy-to-build, complete shelter looking from the front. It is covered with cedar boughs.

dry them if they are wet, in the manner I explained earlier.

It's always good to have something at your back such as boughs or bark for protection from the cold. It's also good to have something to lean against. You only need to build the shelter large enough for your body and high enough so that you are able to sit up in it.

Build your fire directly in front of the opening, close enough so that you can get heat from it while you are inside the opening, but not so close that your shelter is in danger of catching fire.

In many areas you may be able to find a bank or big rock, or even an overhanging ledge that may serve as a shelter, but be sure it isn't something that could cave in on you. Also, if it is raining hard, don't camp in a dry stream bed, or in a low spot in case there is flooding. If there is a lightning storm, don't shelter under a tall tree, as it is more apt to get hit by lightning. You are safer right out in the open. In this type of storm you never want to touch a wire, or go through a wire fence. If you need to go through, lie down and roll under without touching it.

Another way to build a good shelter is to cut a bunch of very slender willow poles. They need to be green so that they will bend into a half hoop. The hoop, at the highest part, should be three to four feet high, which means you need an eight to ten foot pole. If you can't find one that long use whatever is available. It will take two pieces to make one hoop of the shorter length. The shelter should be about four feet wide, and about six feet long.

To make a tool to make holes with, take your hatchet and cut a stick about one and one half inches in diameter, and about 12 to 14 inches long. Cut the top off blunt and sharpen the other end. You can use it as a punch. With the hatchet, drive the punch into the ground about six inches, making each hole about a foot apart, with five holes on each side and two on the back end. Stand one of the willows in a hole and bend it over, sticking the other end in a hole on the opposite side. If the willow poles are short, stand one in each hole, then take and bend both of them over, making a hoop, and tie them at the top part. If you are short of string, just

Emergency shelter or wind break.

wrap the ends around each other. After they are all in place, take some more willows, and space them about 12 inches apart and weave them by going over one hoop and under the next, pushing them all the way through the hoop by going over and under every other one. They should stay in place without having to be tied. You can weave the front part in the same manner, leaving a hole big enough to crawl in. The back end of the shelter doesn't have to be as high as the front. Cover the woven frame with boughs or anything you can find.

You can vary the shape, a round one being a little bit easier to build than a long shape.

Basically the shelter is made in the same manner as an old Indian sweat lodge. If you use it for a sweat lodge, or you want to heat the inside of the shelter, build a fire fairly close to the outside of the doorway. Gather several rocks six to ten inches in diameter, if you can find them, and put them in the fire. Let them heat until they are glowing red hot. Inside the shelter dig a little hole to one side of the doorway. If you can't dig a hole just clean out all the

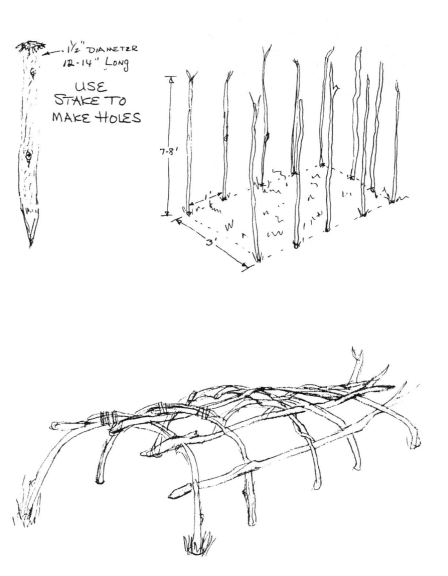

.1½" DIAMETER
12-14" LONG

USE
STAKE TO
MAKE HOLES

7-8'

3'

The framework for a shelter, minus the front end. This shelter is about three and one-half feet high in the front and about one foot high in the back end. This same shelter can be built round instead of long like this one.

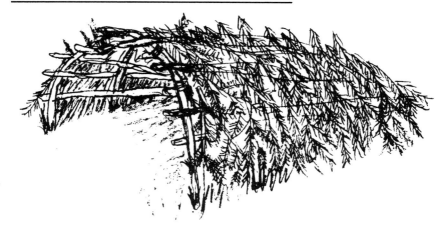

The shelter, covered with boughs. Note how the boughs are placed over the framework to help keep them in place.

vegetation in a space about one and a half to two feet across. Don't leave anything that will burn there or you will have smoke in the shelter. Carry or roll a few rocks into the hole with a forked stick, leaving the rest in the fire for later use. The rocks in the shelter should stay warm for at least three hours. When you go inside close the doorway with boughs. When the rocks cool, return them to the fire, put more hot ones in the hole, and rebuild your fire. You can use this method for any type of shelter.

It's surprising how much body heat you can save by covering up with green boughs. I have been caught many times in freak storms without good enough clothes, and no rain gear, and have had other people with me who weren't properly dressed for the weather. I always carry extra string, cord or wire along, and many times I have stopped along the trail, or out in the woods and cut a few boughs to make a rain cover. Western red cedar boughs that lay flat are best, but I have also used fir. I tie them with the stems up in a fashion to make a good cape to cover my back. If I'm on horseback I cut two bunches, tie them together by the stems and lay them across my horse's neck just in front of the saddle. After mounting, I pull the boughs up over my lap and leave them hanging over my legs like a pair of chaps. You'd be surprised how warm those new chaps and jacket can be. You can also hang some from your waist if you are walking.

When I was a small boy I learned a little trick from the Indian women that I have used ever since. When the bushes or trees were wet with rain or snow, the women would cut or find a stick about four feet long, and use it to knock the moisture off the bushes to keep their long skirts from getting too wet. When on horseback, I use his method to knock the wet off branches hanging in the pathway so that all the water and snow doesn't land in my lap.

When camping out, be sure to take good care of your clothes so that they will last until you get back to civilization. One mistake people make is burning their shoes and garments while trying to dry them out by the fire, because they leave them unattended for a few minutes. Any leather is real sensitive to heat, and I have seen people burn spots on their shoes while they were on their feet. The amount of heat an outdoor fire puts out can change very quickly, and it can be hot on one side and cool on the other. If you hang clothing up to dry, be sure it is far enough from the fire that there is no chance of it burning. I have found that the best and fastest way to dry clothes out is to hold them in your hands and swing them back and forth near the fire. Don't leave any clothing hanging unattended by the fire even for one minute, because it may catch a spark. Even if you are in a tent or cabin with a stove, you want to be careful how close you put your clothes to the fire. Lots of cabins and homes have burned down as a result of clothing catching fire by the stove.

It's important to keep your clothes as dry as possible in cold weather, and if you get into a tight spot think carefully over everything you are going to do before you actually do it. Consider whether it may be a good or bad idea under the circumstances. People sometimes put themselves in more danger of freezing in cold weather by reacting to a bad situation without thinking ahead.

A few years ago, quite late during hunting season, my sons and I were coming down from a real high, remote area where we had been packing some mountain goat out. We were horseback and

In the four photographs on these two pages, the author demonstrates how to construct a simple survival shelter should you become caught out in the woods and need temporary protection from the elements. First comes the framework (top photo), tied together with string or twine, then covering the top with the small tarp you carry in your daybag. Note the rock in the corner of the tarp to hold it in position.

Then cover the tarp and the rest of the shelter with boughs cut-end up so they'll both drain water and provide insulation to keep heat in the shelter. Remember that this is a survival set-up, not one you'll want to utilize except in a survival situation. See finished shelter on next page.

The finished shelter, put up within a half an hour, provides a lean-to canopy under which you can get protection from the elements with your fire pit located immediately in front of the lean-to so the fire will handily warm you.

had some pack stock with us. The weather was nice in the morning, but by midday a very fast storm moved in. A heavy rain started and quickly turned into snow. Then suddenly it became extremely cold. As we came down to the lower part of the mountains in this very remote area, we came across five grown men who were not familiar with this part of the country. None of the men had a hatchet, but all had knives and had worked unsuccessfully at trying to start a fire. They had no tent or shelter, but each had a sleeping bag. All five of them had stripped off every stitch of their soaking-wet clothing and climbed into their sleeping bags. Some of them had hung their wet clothing on bushes or logs, others left their clothes crumpled up on the ground along with their shoes, which were half full of solid ice when we found them. The big game hunters' sleeping bags were already soaking wet and starting to freeze around their bodies. Every piece of their clothing was frozen stiff, and they were 10 or 12 miles from the closest road.

We built a fire and thawed and dried out the clothes, then got the five men out of their sleeping bags and dressed again. We then took them the six miles to our main camp. If we had not happened to find those men when we did, none of them would have been able to get out of their frozen sleeping bags, and even if they had, they couldn't have gotten their solidly frozen clothes on. If only one of these fellows had carried a hatchet and known how to use it, they probably could have gotten a fire going and been alright. We have seen many similar instances where people nearly lost their lives simply because they didn't think to be prepared for an emergency situation.

Emergency shelter or wind break.

SOMEONE HURT OR SICK
IN THE BACK COUNTRY

You may have wondered what you would, or should, do if you were in the wilderness and a partner or someone in your group got seriously hurt, or became ill and needed medical assistance.

First try to remain calm so you can use good judgment. If there are more than two people in your party, someone should stay to tend the injured one while someone else goes for help. If there is no one else with you, first try to make the injured person as comfortable as possible. Take your hatchet and cut a good bed of boughs, and make a little shelter of some kind. If you have any extra clothing that you don't need to wear, use it to cover your partner with. Leave any food or water close enough so that he or she can reach it without moving.

Before you leave, explain what your plans are, and then be very sure that you will be able to find the spot when you return with help. If you are in doubt about finding the place, use your hatchet to blaze both sides of the trees as you leave your partner. If you get to a spot where the trees are far apart, or you don't have a hatchet with you, blaze a trail the way the Indians did when I was a small boy. Break off branches of trees and bushes as you go along, but don't break them off completely. Let each branch hang so it dangles from the bush or tree. If you travel through open area, do the same thing with taller weeds and grass. The hanging branches are much easier to spot than if they are completely broken off. Try to break the branches at eye level if you can, so that they will be easier to see on your return.

When I blaze out to a main trail or road, I break or cut a couple of good-sized green branches for markers and lay them in an easily visible spot on the road at the place where I left the woods. This way anyone can find the place where they should leave the trail or road, even at night if they carry a flashlight or lantern. My boys and guides and I have used boughs as markers on our trails for many different reasons, such as where to turn off to a good fishing hole, a certain ridge or canyon, to a game kill, or maybe just to let someone else in the party know where we left the main trail. You could use a pole or something larger to lay across the trail for a marker, but if someone else comes along they more than likely will throw it off the trail. If you use boughs that lie flat, other trail users aren't likely to bother picking them up.

SOME DANGERS OF MOUNTAIN CLIMBING IN SUMMER

I don't encourage a large group to climb steep mountains or peaks in the same area for two reasons: there's always one or more individuals who want to climb faster than the others, and there's always those who cannot keep up with the group.

The better climbers end up above the slower ones, and there is risk of them dislodging loose rocks which may roll down on the climbers below. If a person accidentally loosens a rock, he or she should try to catch it and stop it from rolling, but sometimes it's not possible to do so, and the rock tumbles down the mountain right onto the person below. In this case, climbing a ravine or draw is much more dangerous than climbing a ridge. If you are on a ridge the rock may go off to one side or the other, but if you are in a ravine, there is nowhere else for the rock to go except down. It may bounce from side to side, but it will still follow the ravine, and anyone below it is in great danger.

If you are going to do any steep climbing with a group of people, I would advise that you make sure that no one lags behind. Keep everyone in a close group, with each person within a step or two of the person ahead. This way if someone knocks a rock loose, somebody close by should be able to catch or deflect the rock before it gathers speed. When stopping a loose rock, put it in a little hole or position it so that it won't get started again. Each person should be very careful and concerned for the person below.

If you are climbing in summer and come across a steep snowfield or glacier, and you don't have snow or ice equipment and are inexperienced, go around it instead of over it. If you do go

Snowfields such as these in the background can be very dangerous and it generally is best to simply stay off them.

out onto a steep ice field and you lose your footing, there is no way that you can stop yourself from sliding, and you will go like lightning. If you come to a spot where there is no other option but to cross, and you don't have an ice axe or pick, then you should at least have your hatchet with you. It's not always possible, but try to find a good, strong stick, cut it about five feet long and sharpen one end. If the snow isn't too hard, you can poke it into the snow with each step that you take for support. Try to get each of your steps into the snow so that you won't slip. If you have to, use your hatchet to cut holes for your steps. If it is hard ice, you are better to stay off of it altogether.

A few years ago we packed in a group of Explorer Scouts and their leaders to the top of the Mission Mountains in Montana with our string of mules. After making camp, I warned all the boys and their leaders about the danger of going onto steep snow fields. On the second day two of the young fellows must have doubted what I told them because they sneaked off from the rest of the group to a snowfield about a mile and a half from camp. They climbed around to the top part of the glacier and thinking it would be great fun, couldn't resist going out on the upper part of it. They had only taken a few steps when they both fell and started sliding. They went so fast that they couldn't slow themselves. One of the boys was lucky because, when he hit the bottom, he slid out where the rocks were small, so he only got skinned up quite badly. The other boy went off the snow head first into some larger rocks and was knocked unconscious. His friend ran to camp for help and we made a stretcher and carried the injured boy back to camp. He came to on the way, but he had split his head open with a gash about four inches long. We had some first-aid spray that deadens pain, needles and stitching material, and one of the other young fellows had some training, so he sewed him up.

Even if something looks like fun, don't take a chance on it, as you may not be so lucky as those two. You may lose your life.

When climbing cliffs, ledges, and peaks, use good judgment. A lot of people, myself and my brothers and sons included, have made some dumb decisions when we climbed into

Even in mid-summer in the Rocky Mountains, you may have to cross over snowfields like this one where extreme caution must be exercised whether you're traveling via foot or horseback. When these snowfields lie on a steep incline, it is impossible to hold your footing on them.

places where we shouldn't have, and were lucky to get out alive. Many people have lost their lives by just getting a little bit careless. Be very sure that you will be able to get back down a cliff you are climbing. When climbing up a cliff, you can see your hand and footholds, but if you keep going over spots like this and then you finally find that you can't go any further and must turn back, as I have done many times in my life, you may not be able to remember exactly where you came up. And on your way down you won't be able to see the hand and footholds that you used on the way up.

Several times I have had an awful feeling in the pit of my stomach when I was trying to find my way back down a cliff, not being sure if I was in the same place or not, and having to feel for footholds. I've known fellows who let themselves down over ledges, and then couldn't get back up, and had to be rescued with ropes. There are too many people doing these kinds of things who end up losing their lives, or cause those rescuing them to lose their lives, so think ahead about the consequences of getting into that kind of situation.

It's wise to take a chalk marker like the kind used for marking logs when you are climbing. Mark your path on the rocks wherever it is particularly difficult to climb, so that you can follow the same path back down.

Drinking Water

When you are vigorously climbing in the mountains, or hiking through the woods, you should start to sweat, as the harder you are working the more your body will sweat. And the more that you sweat the faster your body will need water. Soon you will be getting very thirsty. Therefore, the thirstier you get the faster you will play out or get exhausted and the more you sweat the more water you will need. Consequently, you should carry a canteen full of water with you. And, if you're going to be hiking all day, you may need more than one canteen of water.

In the northwestern states and Canada, I have never found running water in the mountains that was not drinkable, although there could be some in places that I have not been. I have, however, found some water that does not taste as good as others.

If you are climbing high mountains or peaks, you'll discover that the higher you climb the less water you will find. I like to keep my canteen with plenty of water in it to sustain me until I get back to my base camp. While climbing or hunting, I will stop and refill my canteen if I find a good cold spring or stream. If I am not familiar with the water I find I will take a little sip of it to see what it tastes like.

I feel it is safe to drink from nearly all water in this part of the country that is coming out of the rock or ground, and which is flowing freely as there would be little chance of contamination of any kind. However, you should be very careful of drinking any water that is not moving or being fed by a spring or stream. Back

When climbing this type of rugged mountain country, each person in a party should make a mental effort to be extra careful not only because of the difficulty of the terrain and the distance you are from aid, should you need it, but because the loose sedimentary rock poses a double hazard of slipping underfoot or tumbling down onto other hikers. This scene is of McDonald Peak in the Mission Mountains when viewed from the north.

in the 1970's my oldest son took a drink of water from an elk track in the mud that was full of water. He was so thirsty that he laid down and drank the water out of the elk track as he had given all of his water to his hunter, who had not wanted to carry the weight of a canteen. That same evening, my son started to get sick and had to be flown out of the Bob Marshall Wilderness with a sickness just like typhoid fever.

So be very careful of drinking stagnant water. If it is not running and has green moss on it, be very careful. Simply do not drink it no matter how thirsty you might be.

CROSSING A STREAM OR SMALL RIVER

If you need to cross a stream and there is no bridge to cross on, you can usually find a logjam at some point if you are in a timbered area, and cross on that. Or you may find a spot where the creek is narrow enough that you can throw some logs across. You may even find a big log lying across the stream. If you feel that you are not steady enough to walk across the log, find a slender pole long enough to reach down in the stream bottom, and use it to steady yourself while walking the log. If the log is slick or wet, straddle it and scoot yourself across. Don't take any chances; a wet log is dangerous. Many times I have vaulted across a stream with a pole. Before you try it, try your pole out on the ground to make sure it is strong enough to hold your weight. If it breaks on you over the stream, not only will you get wet, but you risk the danger of running a sharp point into your body.

If there is no other way to get across a large stream or small river but to ford it, remember that rivers or streams that don't have a fine, gravelly or sandy bottom will almost always be very slippery. If the rocks on the bottom are slick, it will be harder to hold your footing if you are barefooted. Usually we don't want to get our shoes and clothes wet, but if you have to cross a fairly wide span of water, I would suggest that you at least keep your shoes on so you don't slip so bad.

If you take the rest of your clothes off, put your socks in your pants pocket and save out a piece of string. Lay your shirt out on the ground with both sleeves stretched out. Roll the rest of your clothes up in your pants, then lay the bundle on the inside part of your shirt between the sleeve holes. Button the shirt up over the rest of your clothing, take the shirt tail and roll it up over the rest of the cloth, and take your string and tie it so that the bundle will not unroll. Take up your shirt by both the sleeves and put one of the sleeves from your back over one shoulder. Bring the other sleeve from the back up under the opposite arm. (Don't tie the bundle around your neck, or you will end up choking.) Tie the two sleeves together in front of you.

Before you tie your clothes on, find yourself a slender but stout pole, one that is not too hard to handle. Sharpen the bottom end. If the water is good and clear, it may be a little deeper than it looks. If the water is muddy or murky so that you can't see the bottom, find a place where there are riffles all the way across the river or stream. This is usually the shallowest part of the stream, so if you stay just a few feet above the riffles, you will have a good place to cross. When you start across where the water starts to get swift, take your pole and stick the sharp end into the water a short way below your body and brace yourself against the pole. Be careful not to step in a deep hole. If the water starts to get up to the lower part of your body and if it is at all swift, it may be better to turn back, because it will be extremely difficult to keep your footing at that depth. Also, remember that if the water is very cold your legs can cramp so badly that you may not be able to move them. People have been known to drown in knee-deep water for this reason.

Once you get across the stream, take off your shoes, turn them upside down, and leave them until they quit dripping. Then put them on with your dry socks and they will finish drying on your feet. The rest of your clothes should be dry enough to put on.

If the water crossing doesn't look good to you, don't try it! Life is too precious to risk losing it just to get across a stream or river. A stream or river with a gravelly bottom can change from year to year, and where it may have had a nice flat bottom last time you crossed, the next year after high water it may be completely different.

FINDING FOOD IN AN EMERGENCY SITUATION

There are lots of wild plants that can be eaten if you run out of food. For example, grasses like timothy, fescue, and brome are edible.

If the plant isn't too ripe you can pull the joints apart, and if they slip apart easily, the ends are nice and soft so you can chew them right up. If the heads are partly formed and still in the boot, pull them out and eat them.

I eat a lot of clover and alfalfa, blossom and plant both. These plants can be found along nearly all trails where there have been horses, and most plants that horses eat we can eat also. Thistles, such as bull thistle and elk thistle are very good if you peel the stems and eat the inside. The blossom is also tasty.

There are a lot of different berries that can be eaten, but they get scarcer after a frost hits. Rosehips hang on late and are good to eat, and kinnickinick berries stay on all winter. Kinnickinick is a low growing bush about four to six inches long and produces small, round, red berries which are a little chalky, but edible. I have eaten the tips off of snowbrush.

If you are in country where there are pine nuts, you'll find that they make a very good meal. Ponderosa Pine nuts are good, but very small. Huckleberries, serviceberries, raspberries and thimbleberries grow in the mountains and are all good to eat.

Lots of wild plants are good, but don't eat anything that you don't know, because some are poisonous. It is difficult to describe which plants to eat without illustrations, so I suggest anyone planning to go into the backcountry get a book on edible plants of the region and either take it along or study it before

One of the reasons you carry a piece of wire in your daybag is so you can, should an emergency need develop, make a loop snare with it for catching fish, birds or small animals. You can use a pole with a stout end or a flexible one, as demonstrated here. The close-up of the snare end shows how to form the loop at the end of the snare.

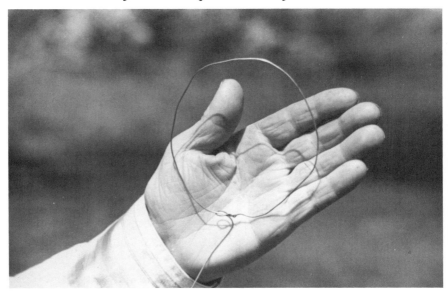

starting out.

I got into the habit of carrying a piece of copper wire with me when I was a small boy going to school in the 1920's. I was from a family of 13 children and my parents barely had enough money for the essentials, so we had to earn our own spending money. The only way I could earn money at the time was to use copper wire to snare trout and whitefish from the streams that ran through our valley, and sell them to a few steady customers who lived in town eight miles away.

The best wire that I found came from the old Model T Ford car coils. The copper wire was just the right size, smooth and tough, and it was a nice bright color. I figured out many other uses for this wire, and even now I like to carry a piece in my pocket when going out in the backcountry.

If you are in a survival situation and desperate for food,

The author demonstrates the use of the wire snare in a small stream. The trick is to ease the loop around a fish, working from downstream up and then jerking the loop tight when you get it in position.

Most of the streams and lakes in the Rocky Mountains support native cutthroat trout like this one that can be caught with a hook and line, or a snare wire in an emergency. It's best to carry both in the "emergency kit" you keep in your daybag

and you don't have a hook and line, you can use a piece of copper wire to snare fish. If there is a stream or river near, find the deeper, quieter holes. Sneak up to the holes cautiously, because any quick movement will scare the fish. Usually they will be within an inch or two of the bottom when they aren't feeding. Once you've located a fish, cut a long, slender pole from willow or some other type of supple wood. Take out your wire and make a very small loop on one end of it, then run the other end through the loop. Back the copper wire back a little way, just enough to make another loop a little larger around than the fish.

You want the loop to go over and around the fish easily, without touching it. Fasten the wire at the tip of the small end of the pole. I use two half hitches, leaving about 14 to 16 inches between the big loop and the end of the pole. Stretch the excess copper wire down the pole and tie the end as far down as you can. This way, if the end of your pole breaks and you have a fish on, you won't lose the wire or the fish.

Sneak back to the pool where the fish are with the wire and loop straight out from the end of the post. I bend the wire slightly at the edge of the loop to help keep the loop open. Insert the pole into the water very gently until the wire is almost touching the bottom. The reason the copper wire works so well for a snare is because it is flexible and shiny if you keep it cleaned, and you can see it well enough to keep it where you want it. Move the pole and wire downstream as gently as possible. When you are close to the fish, the wire should be barely touching the bottom.

Without touching the fish, ease the wire around its body. Once you have the wire past the gills, or to the front fins, or just past the front fins, give him a quick jerk and you've got him. If the fish starts to move when you get past the gills, you'd better jerk or he will be gone through the wire.

If there aren't any fish to catch, you can get grouse using the same method. Slip the loop over their heads. Franklin grouse, also known as the fool's hen, are real easy to catch this way. Ruffed grouse are harder to catch, but quite often blue grouse are easy.

When the squirrels are gathering their cones, it's easy to get them by putting the snare in their runways as they travel back and forth with cones, and you can snare rabbits the same way. However, I don't encourage anyone to snare a fish or other animal unless you are lost and in extreme need of food.

If you have killed game and don't have a pan to cook it in, cut a green stick about three feet long, big enough to hold up anything that you are going to put on it. Sharpen both ends of the stick and poke it through the fish or other animal. With the meat on one end of the stick, punch the other end of the stick into the ground at the edge of the fire, just far enough from the fire so it won't burn. Put it in the ground at an angle so that the meat hangs over the fire a little. Turn the meat half way around now and then so that it will cook evenly. Don't try to rush it; let it cook slowly.

Another way is to cut two forked sticks and sharpen the other end of each so they can be stuck into the ground, one on each side of the fire. Then cut another stick long enough to reach from one fork to the other, and hang your meat on it over the fire to cook.

In the early days when I used to hunt with the Indians in the backcountry and we killed something large, like a moose, or if we killed several elk, we would move the camp to the kill, instead of bringing the meat to the camp. The only time the meat was brought into camp was when it was a deer, or a small enough animal that we could get it onto a horse or drag it into camp. On most of the hunting trips there were more women than there were men, as the women were needed to take care of the meat.

Very little meat was ever brought out fresh. Instead, a frame was built with four poles that were driven into the ground. The poles were spaced far enough apart to make whatever size rack was needed to dry the meat on. Two poles were tied on, one at each end, and several little poles were then spaced apart on the top. The animals were skinned right there, and the meat cut off the bones in chunks. They would cut around and around each piece of meat, sometimes ending up with a thin slab of meat two feet long. The thin slabs of meat dried quickly. It was hung on the racks about four feet above the fire and dried until it was sort of crispy.

Wood that was free of pitch, such as alder and aspen was burned, rather than conifers which are pitchy. The pitch will stick to the meat, giving it a bad flavor, and will turn the meat black. If the meat was to be stored for a long period of time, the Indians would dry it without salting it, because the salt would draw moisture, causing the meat to mildew in storage.

To make a drying frame, get four poles about five feet long for the uprights, and sharpen one end of each pole. Drive each post in the ground, forming a square. Cut four more poles and tie them to the posts about four feet above the ground. If you don't have enough string or wire, cut strips of the skin to tie it up with. Then cut enough smaller poles to lay across the frame so that the meat or fish can be hung on them. Start a fire under the meat with

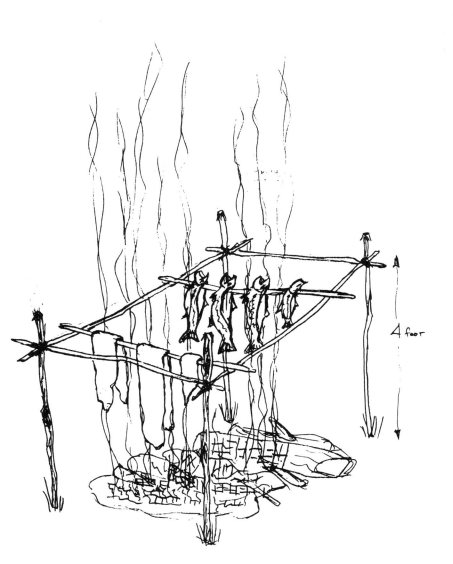

Meat and fish are being dried, Indian style, on this frame.

wood that isn't pitchy. Don't build the fire too large, or you may burn the meat.

Wild Plants That Can Be Eaten

Should you need to do so, it's perfectly safe to eat some wild plants and listed below are a few commonly-available edible plants. But be very careful because there are many wild plants that are poisonous — so be sure of what you are eating. These plants are edible:

1. Dandelion — the tender part of the plant and yellow blossom.

2. Cattails — any tender part and the roots.

3. Wild onions — the bulb and the stems.

4. Bitterroots, watercress and clover of all kinds — the blossom and leaves are all edible.

5. Thistles of different kinds — the tender inner parts and blossoms.

If you are lost you may not have a cooking kettle. But if you have a way to make a tea you can use the inner bark of trees such as birch, fir, spruce, hemlock, pine, poplar, aspen, cottonwood, huckleberry leaves, fireweed, mint, nettles, willow leaves and bark. Also the tips off snowbrush can be boiled or eaten raw. All of these will make good tea.

We have a lot of good, edible mushrooms, but we also have a lot of poisonous ones, so be sure that you know the good ones before you eat them.

If you or anyone with you should eat anything that is poisonous you should immediately induce vomiting. Salt water (one pint) is good. Gag with a finger. Mustard water (one pint). You can use charcoal from the campfire. Smash or grind it into a cup of water so you can drink it.

Most of the water in the Northwest is drinkable, although there have been some cases of giardia. If you are able to find springs or water that has just come out of the ground, has not run very far, or run through any stagnant water, you are generally safe in drinking the water.

Meats

If you want to keep your strength, I think a source of meat is good — but sometimes it is hard to get. I believe that big game animals are the best but sometimes you have to take whatever you can get — such as frogs, turtles, fish, squirrels, mice, rats, porcupines, or snakes. Any kinds of birds can also be eaten. Meat can be eaten raw, but, for my part, I like to cook all of my meat.

THINGS THE HUNTER SHOULD KNOW

Fall or Winter Wear/Hunting Items for Ten Days.
Here is a list of cold weather clothing a hunter should have:
1. Underwear: three pairs with one pair shorts and top. One pair of medium weight 50% wool long johns. One pair 80-100% wool long johns.
2. Socks: use a type with soft, fine weave, two pair light or medium-light, two pair of medium-heavy wool socks, one pair of heavy wool socks.
3. Shirts: you will need one cotton shirt and 2 wool shirts.
4. Pants: one pair light pants and one pair light weight all wool pants. Also, one pair heavy all wool pants.
5. Jackets: one light wool jacket or sweater, one heavy wool jacket, one set of rain gear of good quality.
6. Foot wear: One pair leather boots with eight-inch tops, and one pair of rubber boots with 12-inch tops. Make sure both have good traction soles.
7. Head wear: At least one good cap with earflaps. It is wise to bring a stocking cap to wear to sleep during cold weather.
8. Hand wear: one pair of leather mittens with wool lining, two pairs of wool gloves, one pair of leather or cotton gloves.
Note: There are new types of outdoor clothing on the market today that I know nothing about which may be very good, so check with your sporting goods stores.
As you can see, I encourage the use of wool clothing. Wool has been used for a long time, and I feel it is superior in warmth to anything else I have tried. Wool will keep you warm even if you get soaking wet, and the soft fibers are not noisy in the

You can encounter weather like this anytime in the late fall and early winter through the Rocky Mountain high country and have to be prepared for it whether you're on horseback or afoot. Good clothing is essential if you plan to be out in the wilderness at this time of year.

woods, which is important for stalking game. Most other fabrics will let the cold penetrate through to your body when wet, and will also become noisy in the woods.

If you are hunting, avoid wearing any clothing that will make a swishing noise when walking, as the sound is very foreign to all wild animals, and it will alert them to your presence. Wool is also good because it is not highly flammable, and it won't melt onto your skin if a spark flies onto it like some of the newer outdoor clothing made out of synthetic material.

The Behavior of Wild Animals

I have spent all of my life of 81 years in the woods working, hunting, fishing and mountain climbing and I have never, ever felt concerned about any danger from any of the wild animals in any part of the Rocky Mountains. Many, many times I have camped overnight right in the center of grizzly bear areas, where fresh tracks and droppings, and also fresh diggings, were all over. I also knew that there were mountain lions in the same area. And I never worried about being attacked by any of them. This was back when there were many more grizzly bears than there are today. In my past years it seemed like every wild animal I saw was doing its very best to get away from me.

Although I have always been cautious of surprising an old sow grizzly with cubs, as I know they are very protective of their young. But now, do you know what, I am changing my mind just a little bit. I do not know if it is my age of 81 years or if I am not as active as I once was. In my lifetime I have seen no more than a dozen lions in the wild, although, while hunting them with our lion dogs, I have seen many of them after they were treed by the dogs. The lion is a very sneaky animal. You can be where you know they are there but still you rarely see one of them.

One time I was high in the Mission Mountain Wilderness. I had gotten off my saddle horse which was a big, fine, black horse. With my sharp axe in one hand, I was leading my horse with the other hand. I was going along and cutting little trees and brush that had started to grow into the edges of the horse trail. As I went along cutting stuff out of the trail, I knew there was something behind us as my horse kept turning his head one way and then the other way and looking over his back. I stopped to look several times but didn't see anything.

I went along for about two miles and had just come down off a fairly steep hill when I looked back, just in time, to see the cat about 50 yards back up the trail. He crouched down in the trail and was almost invisible. If I hadn't looked when I did, I would never have seen him. He must have followed me for about two miles before I finally saw him, although my horse knew all along that the cat was there. A horse has excellent vision. My belief is that these cats that follow you are just curious. That has always been my belief.

From the early 1920's to the 1950's there were no

restrictions on hunting the mountain lions. And we, along with a lot of other people, hunted them just for the bounty which kept them down in population about like they should have been. But since there has been a regular season on them they have multiplied tremendously and — it seems — since then they have become more aggressive.

In all the years that I have been in the mountains, whenever I got tired, or at lunch time, I would always lay down under a tree or just out on the ground, usually on my jacket. My five sons and their sons have all done the same thing. After relaxing and taking a nap I always felt that I was then good for a long ways again. Last fall (1995), during the elk hunting season in the Bob Marshall Wilderness, one of my grandsons, Micky, who is in his mid 20's, encountered a mountain lion in such a situation.

While guiding a group of hunters they discovered a bunch of elk in a heavily wooded canyon that was difficult to hunt, so the guides were going to sit a hunter down on each of the game trails that led out of this heavy wooded canyon. Then all the guides would try to drive the elk out to the hunters. Micky had 45 minutes to wait before the drive was to start as the guides had to get their hunters all placed on the game trails. So, Mick decided to take a nap while he waited.

The timber was very heavy all around him. He laid down and went to sleep. Something startled him out of his sleep. He thought some elk were going by him, so he jumped up quickly and, lo and behold, there was a big cougar crouched about seven or eight feet in front of him. It scared Micky so bad that he threw his arms up and hollered at it. This must have startled the big cat. It jumped up onto a log; then two more cats jumped up onto the same log. He also heard some brush crack behind him but didn't see what was there. He was not even carrying a gun with him. It scared him so bad that he said he will never take another nap in cougar country. I think the rest of the family, including myself, will be more cautious from now on. I do believe that if he had not awakened when he did and jumped and startled the lion, he may have been a goner.

I feel that it was a good thing that he did not try to run from them; if he had run, they would have had him. In all our years of being around the mountain lion as long as the man or dogs are the aggressor, I feel you are quite safe. I don't feel that any person should ever run from one of them or they would have you so quick as all of their prey are always trying to get away from them.

I feel that the mountain lion and the grizzly bear are the only two wild animals that people have to be concerned about. The lions have multiplied so fast in the last few years, and a lot of them are living in so close to people, that they are losing all of their fear of man and are starting to get more aggressive. As for the grizzly bears, they are a long ways down in numbers but it seems they are also getting more aggressive than they once were.

It seems to me that most of the problem bears are in the national parks or are bears that have been transferred from the parks to other areas. I believe that a lot of the "park bears" get aggressive because most people that see a bear will throw their lunch to the bear, and then run away. The bears learn real fast that if they run after someone they will get a hand-out and they do continue to get bolder all the time. The bears in the back country did not seem to be aggressive, but nowadays there may be transplanted bears from the parks in any of the areas. So everyone needs to be more careful than we used to have to be.

I have been packing into the Bob Marshall and Mission Mountain Wilderness, where there are a lot of grizzly bears, since 1924. In all of these years, I never had to kill even one grizzly that got into my camp. And no one has ever been hurt, over all those years, by one in our parties or camps. It may be that we have just been lucky, but I still advise anyone to still be cautious while going into the back country.

SHOOTING GAME

I have read a lot of hunting stories and heard a lot of supposedly big game hunters say that the best way to shoot grizzly, elk or moose is to shoot them in the shoulders and break them down. Well, I've shot my share of big game, and I have seen hundreds of big game animals being shot. I would never encourage anyone to shoot any animal in the shoulders, for though you may break one shoulder, you are very unlikely to break the other one.

Any animal is able to travel a long distance with a broken shoulder, and besides, there is no vital spot on the shoulder except for the arteries, and chances are the animal will not die for a long time. Besides that there is a lot of good meat on the shoulder that you don't want to waste. I always encourage my hunters to shoot their animal just behind the shoulders, and, looking at it up and down, just a little below center. This way you are sure to hit the heart, liver, or lungs. The animal may not fall instantly, but it will not go very far before it falls.

It has been a very few times that I have had to shoot an animal with more than one shot. If an animal is shot too high, like from the backbone down about eight inches the full length of the animal, there is nothing vital. This is why a lot of hunters lose their game. Of course a good spinal shot will put the game down, but you will have to finish it off.

Some hunters believe that because they have big, high powered rifles they can hit an animal anywhere and it will go right down. Not true. An elk, especially, will go quite a distance before it falls, and quite often, if the hunter doesn't see it go down, he won't bother to go look for it.

If an animal is hit but keeps on going, I will sit down and

have a sandwich or take a nap, waiting at least half an hour before going to look for it. Usually the animal won't go far before lying down if you don't go after it too quickly. It will be watching for you and if it sees you coming, it will keep running. But if you wait about thirty minutes the animal will forget about you, and if you are real careful you may be able to get quite close to it before it will try to get away. You should move very slowly and search carefully because game animals are hard to find when they are lying down.

It's easy to tell when a deer is hit because it almost always drops or tucks its tail, and sometimes it will hunch up. However, it's very difficult to tell if an elk has been hit. If an animal isn't killed on the spot, it's a good idea to mentally mark the area where it was shot before you go over there. Otherwise you may have trouble finding the exact spot and its tracks.

If an animal is shot a little too high in the body, it may not bleed at all on the outside, especially if the bullet hits a bone and doesn't go all the way through. I have even trailed animals that have been shot clear through up to a quarter of a mile before I found any blood, and sometimes I found the animal dead.

When traveling on foot, I carry my hatchet in a sheath which hangs from my belt. If I am traveling horseback, I hang my hatchet from the saddle horn and tie it down. That way, if I need to cut a pole or some brush from the trail I have it handy for quick use. For setting up a larger camp, or a hunting camp, my family and I use larger axes, but the hatchet is always handy to use for driving stakes and nails, and for cutting kindling.

A hatchet is a must on an elk hunt, and we encourage every one of our hunters to carry one. If an elk, moose, or any large animal is killed, it is almost impossible to clean out the animal properly without a hatchet. When an animal is killed, it should be cleaned as quickly as possible, taking all of the entrails out, including the gullet and windpipe. If the animal has been shot in the chest cavity, it's usually not necessary to cut its throat, because the blood is usually all in the chest cavity. If you aren't saving the cape for mounting, you may as well cut the throat, or stick it in

Caring for game often must be done in surroundings that make cleaning out and skinning the animal difficult, as is the case with this bull elk taken in dense timber in the Bob Marshall Wilderness.

the chest just in front of the brisket.

When cleaning the animal, I try to get it flat on its back. If I am alone, this is one place where a rope is needed. I always have one on my belt, and some small rope or cord in my pocket. I get the animal into the position that I want in order to work on it, then I tie a foot to a tree or bush. Sometimes I tie two of the feet to hold it in the proper position.

If the animal is not to be caped, I will take my knife and insert the blade under the skin at the neck near the head. I always try to make the cut straight and smooth by cutting from the underside to the outside of the skin, and I cut in the same direction as the hair lies, so as to cut very few of the hairs. If you cut a lot of the hair, it will get on your meat and will be hard to clean off.

If the animal is a male, cut the skin alongside or over the penis all the way to the rectum. Then, staying about one inch away from the rectum, cut the skin all the way around the rectum. Insert the knife blade full length under the rectum and against the rump bone, being very careful and keeping the knife blade pointed a little bit outward, so that you don't cut an intestine. Keeping the knife along the outside part of the pelvic area, cut up both sides, then go back and cut the penis loose from the belly. Then bringing the penis to the back end, lay it out so its end doesn't touch any part of the meat, in case there is any leakage of urine. The critical part comes when you get to the pelvic area. The penis is fastened tight to the back of the pelvic bone, so when you cut it loose, be sure not to insert your knife too deeply, as the blade is very close to the bladder, and if you cut into it you will contaminate the meat with urine. Be sure not to cut the penis off, or again you will end up with urine all over the meat.

When cutting on the rear end, like around the rectum, it will help you a lot if the back end of the animal is uphill, because it will relieve the pressure on the entrails, which have a tendency to want to go toward the front part of the animal. This will make the job a lot easier, and you'll be less apt to cut through an intestine.

When I am finished with the back end, if it's possible, I like to turn the animal with the rump downhill. If it's a large animal you may not be able to turn it, and will have to do the job as best you can. Now is when the hatchet is needed. Anyone who is with you should also have a hatchet.

First, with a knife, cut through the meat to the bone on both the brisket and the pelvis. Then take the two hatchets and split the brisket by pounding one hatchet through, using the other hatchet as a hammer. If you don't have a second hatchet, you can use a rock to pound with, or you may just have to chop through it. I don't like to do this because it makes too many bone chips.

Then move to the pelvis and do the same thing. The pelvis has a bone seam in the very center, so if you get your hatchet started in that seam it will split easily. Do not try to use your knife to split the brisket or pelvis on a large animal; nine times out of ten, you will end up breaking the blade.

Having the animal flat on its back shifts the weight of the intestines toward the bottom of the cavity, relieving the pressure on the diaphragm and belly tissue. Taking your knife at the brisket, cut through the diaphragm and insert two fingers under the tissue, pulling the meat up away from the entrails. With the other hand, use the tip of the knife blade to start cutting right between your two fingers of the other hand, cutting in an outward direction all the way back to the pelvis.

Be careful here, as the entrails are very close to the outside. When the pelvic bone is cut, it should spread open one or more inches between the bone. The front part of the pelvic bone goes quite deep, so you will have to cut deeply into that one spot for it to flop apart.

Now, to remove the entrails I like to have the rump downhill if possible, working from the front end down to the back. I will take the windpipe and the gullet in my left hand, while I cut it loose with the other hand. Cut the diaphragm, a thin layer of meat that separates the heart, liver, and lungs from the rest of the intestines, all the way around on both sides to the backbone. You will have to cut a little along the backbone as you pull the intestines toward the back end.

If someone is with me, I let him do the pulling and I do the cutting. I don't cut the heart and liver away from the intestines until I have them out of the animal. Now I go from one leg to the other, holding them up as I work each leg up and down and around, so that if there is any blood left in the arteries it will come out. If there is excess blood I scoop it out as best I can with my hand.

When I hunt, I like to carry a few sheets of paper towels in my pocket to wipe the excess blood out of the cavity. Then, if there is snow or water I wash my hands. If not, I clean them as best I can with a piece of toweling saved for that purpose. If a person has any scratches or cuts on his hand, it's important to wash them as soon as possible, as infection can set in easily from the blood of the animal.

If I am going to drag an animal very far, I will not use the method of cleaning I described above as the first method. Instead, I roll my shirt sleeves as high as possible and cut a hole in the belly just large enough to get the entrails out. With my knife in one hand, I reach up through the cavity carefully, because I am working in the blind, and when I find the diaphragm I cut through it, all the way from the brisket around the upper part of the rib cage, as far back as I can reach. Then I reach as far up in the neck as I can, cutting off the windpipe and the gullet. and pull them down toward the hole that I have made. With my knife hand I cut the rest of the diaphragm off, starting at the backbone and following the contour of the ribs on the underside.

After cutting the diaphragm all the way around, you should be able to pull that part of the entrails out through the cavity hole. Now go to the back end and cut the rectum as was described before. With one hand shove the rectum all the way through the pelvic area to the inside. Then go back to the belly hole, and reach in and take hold of the back intestines and pull them out through the hole, and there you've got it! You may have to do a little minor cutting while you are pulling.

Turn the animal onto its belly and let the excess blood drain out. If the ground is bare of snow, I take a piece of string from my pocket,and with my knife, punch a few holes at the edge of the entrance to the cavity, cutting through the hide where I took out the entrails. Then I sew the hole back up with the string or cord to keep dirt and debris from getting inside the animal.

Once you have dragged the animal to wherever you are going, you can open it up in the manner described earlier. Remember that your animal should cool as quickly as possible. And also remember that the quicker you skin it, the easier it is to skin.

The best time to skin it is when the carcass is still warm, but I would advise not to skin it if you are planning to leave it in the woods overnight. If I am leaving the animal in the woods, and if I have time to do it, I like to skin the legs a short way, as it is so much easier to do when the body is still warm. I start about six inches below the knee and the hock, and slit the skin to about six inches above the knee and hock. I skin all the way around the joints, exposing all of the joint. Below the joint the skin can be cut all the way around the leg.

Cutting the legs off seems to be difficult for lots of people. Most seem to want to cut too high in the joint, so remember to always cut at the lower part of the joint. If you cut a little bit lower than you think you should, you will be more apt to hit the right spot. Cut all the way around the leg, and be sure to cut all the tendons. You should then be able to twist the leg right off, and with a little practice you will find it very easy to do. Be sure you don't cut the hamstrings in the back of the hind legs, as you will need those to hang up the back quarters.

If you shoot an animal be sure you gut it out as soon as possible. Never leave it uncleaned overnight, or by morning it will smell real bad. The blood and guts in the cavity spoil and produce a gas in a very short time.

If you leave the animal in the woods on the ground overnight, an elk or large animal will not cool out even if there is snow on the ground, especially in the neck and shoulder area, because the thick, insulated hair will keep it from cooling. So, if you aren't able to hang it or get it over a log you may have to drag it to a decent spot to leave it. If the weather is warm, try to drag it into the shade. Gather a few pieces of short logs or poles, or even flat rocks, or anything that you can make a bed out of. Lay the poles or logs parallel to each other about two feet apart, and about the length of the animal. You want these poles to be crossways under the animal. Next, drag or roll the animal onto this bed. It's important that the carcass is off the ground so that air can get all the way around it, allowing it to cool completely. The carcass needs to be on its back with the legs straight up.

Now cut or break a stick about six inches long and prop it between the brisket so that it will be held apart for better cooling. If we are going to pack the animal out with horses or mules, I put both front legs and hind legs in the same position. I may have to use some rope or cord to tie it up in the right position. When it cools, it will be stiff, so when it is quartered for packing out, the quarters will be shaped the same, making them easier to pack out. Before leaving the animal, it's necessary to use that precious hatchet again. I like to find a little bushy tree about five or six feet tall, chop it off, and give it a good shaking to remove all the dead needles, because they are hard to pick off if they fall onto the meat. Lay this little tree tight over the cavity to keep the birds or ravens from getting to the meat. If you don't have a little tree, use fir limbs, or even brush. If you can't find anything to cover it with and there are ravens or other birds around, it may be better to lay the animal on its stomach to protect the meat, as a bunch of birds can eat up an animal in a few hours. However, in this position the carcass won't cool as well.

Drag the entrails a little distance from the carcass. The animals or birds will eat those first. If you leave something like a piece of a garment with your scent on it over the animal, or if you urinate somewhere near the carcass, it will help keep animals such as coyotes away from the meat.

If you should make your kill in a thickly wooded area and you have any doubts about finding it again, you can blaze a route with your hatchet from the kill to a spot that you are sure you can find again. Make your blazes on both sides of the tree about eye level. You need not cut all the way through the bark on larger trees. Make the blazes so that they can be seen by looking from one to another.

If I plan to return with horses or mules, I will blaze a route which the pack animals will be able to get through. Nowadays ribbon can be used for blazes so that the trees aren't permanently marked, but I always take it back off after using it, as I don't like the looks of ribbon all over the woods. Cut the bright colored ribbon in six-inch long pieces and tie each piece with an over-hand blow knot on the end of the limbs or trees as close to eye level as possible. Then when you are finished using them you can take them off again easily on your way out.

A lot of people don't like the taste of wild meat. I think the main reason people find the taste too strong is because the meat wasn't taken care of properly and the flavor tainted. The animal may have been gut-shot, or the intestines or bladder may have been punctured, or the meat may have been half spoiled by the time it was brought home, all of which can affect the flavor of the meat. Most wild meat is very tasty if properly cared for.

HOW MEAT IS PACKED

It takes two mules to pack out one mature elk. We try to take the mules out to the kill and tie them close enough so that they can see us working on the kill. This gives them a chance to get used to the sight and smell of the meat and blood.

Usually, and especially in warmer weather when the flies are still out, we will skin the animal all the way out while it is lying on the ground. It's easier to skin an animal while it is lying flat, than when it is hanging.

When skinning, lay the skin out on all sides of the animal, and keep it as clean as possible. Take a good, sharp axe and split the animal full length right through the backbone. If you are good with an axe, you can do it almost as well as you could with a saw, and a lot faster than with a saw. Separate the hind quarters from the front. We usually cut by leaving one or two ribs attached to the hind quarter.

We have each of our hunters bring white muslin bags which are about three feet by four feet, and which have a tight weave in the cloth so that a fly cannot lay its eggs between the threads. We put each quarter in a bag, lay it on a manty, and then manty it up.

This means that each quarter is laid on a heavy tarp about seven by seven feet in size, and wrapped and tied securely with a rope. Then one quarter is placed on each side of the mule, with the front quarters on one mule and the hindquarters on another.

If you are saving the heart and liver, they can be put in another sack and tied between two quarters on the mule. The cape and skin are put in a feed bag. The horns can be sawed or chopped off of the head, but still attached to part of the skull, and packed over the top of the meat on the mules.

Often wild game such as an elk will be taken in some of the most remote, steep and heavily-timbered country that you can find, and you'll have to transport the game through that sort of terrain to get it out of the back country.

If you kill a trophy animal and you want to have it mounted, be sure that you do not cut the skin on the underside of the neck. Take the cape off by starting half way in between the horns. Your knife needs to be good and sharp to do this.

Remember to cut in the direction that the hair lays, staying on the very top of the neck. Cut in as straight a line as you can to the top of the shoulders, then go down both sides to the front edge of the shoulders to the brisket. Now you can skin the neck and head out, leaving as little meat as possible on the skin. In skinning the head, cut from horn to horn, not too far forward, because you don't want the cut to be seen when mounted. Cut around each horn, taking care to leave all the hair that you can on the hide.

When you get to the ear sockets, cut deep enough so that you don't cut the hide. Be very careful when you get to the eyes.

One of the best ways to pack an elk is to quarter the animal, put each quarter in white muslin bags to protect the meat and then wrap each quarter with a manty (7x7-foot canvas tarps) so they can be packed out on a horse or mule. This keeps the meat clean and protects it from any form of contamination. In some cases, like that shown in this photograph of a nine-point bull elk being brought out of the wilderness, a separate pack animal is needed just to haul the set of antlers.

Go clear to the eyeballs, but be sure not to cut the eyelids. On elk and some deer there is a deep indentation or hole just below the eye. Take a look at it when you cut, or else you may cut across it, leaving a hole in the hide. In that particular spot you have to go deep with the knife. When getting to the nose and lips, be careful to skin past the hair line, leaving part of the lips and nostrils with the skin.

Many hunters cannot get the heads mounted because the cape has been ruined, or it has spoiled. When the weather is warm be sure to salt the cape and hide as soon as possible. Rub a good layer of salt on all parts of the flesh side of the cape or skin. Then roll it up tightly and lay it up on a log or something off the ground. Leave it for 24 hours. The salt will pull the glue and moisture out of the hide. Now unroll it and hang it up in a shady spot and let it drip and dry. Don't leave it rolled up too long or the hair may slip on it.

If the weather happens to be cold, just let the skins freeze without salting them, and keep them frozen until you get them to the taxidermist.

If we are not taking the meat out to a meat processor right away, we keep it in main camp for a few days. We un-manty the heavy tarps, and trim out any parts that are bloodshot where the quarters were shot through. If you don't cut out these parts the meat will spoil a lot faster. When finished, leave the muslin bags tied tightly at the end so that flies can't get in. You can be sure that if there is one little hole left the flies will find it and lay their eggs on the meat.

Hang the meat in a good shady spot on a pole long enough so that a bear can't reach it. If it rains, cover the meat with plastic or tarps, as the rain will cause the meat to spoil faster. If you follow these steps you can be sure to bring your meat out of the woods in clean, fresh condition.

CONCLUSION

Whether hunting, fishing, backpacking or simply day hiking in the woods, it always pays to plan ahead for possible problems, and to know how to take care of yourself in an emergency situation. At the very least it can mean the difference between spending a miserable time in the woods or a relatively comfortable one, at most it can mean the difference between life and death. I hope that the contents of this book are of some value to the reader. I would be very pleased if the tips I offer help save someone's life. I hope those of you who have read this book will act responsibly when you go into the backcountry, and will show yourselves to be good, reliable outdoorsmen and women. Have fun and be careful.

Thank you.

LISTING OF BOOKS

Additional copies of **THE WOODSMAN AND HIS HATCHET,** *and many other of Stoneydale Press' books on outdoor recreation, big game hunting, or historical reminisces centered around the Northern Rocky Mountain region, are available at many book stores and sporting goods stores, or direct from Stoneydale Press. If you'd like more information, you can contact us by calling a Toll Free number,* **1-800-735-7006,** *or by writing the address at the bottom of the page. Here's a partial listing of some of the books that are available:*

Cookbooks

Camp Cookbook, *Featuring Recipes for Fixing Both at Home and in Camp, With Field Stories by Dale A. Burk, 216 pages, comb binding*

Cooking for Your Hunter, *By Miriam Jones, 180 pages, comb binding*

Historical Reminisces

Indian Trails & Grizzly Tales, *By Bud Cheff Sr., 212 pages, available in clothbound and softcover editions.*

They Left Their Tracks, *By Howard Copenhaver, Recollections of Sixty Years as a Wilderness Outfitter, 192 pages, clothbound or softcover editions (One of our all-time most popular books.)*

More Tracks, *By Howard Copenhaver, 78 Years of Mountains, People & Happiness, 180 pages, clothbound or softcover editions.*

Copenhaver Country, *By Howard Copenhaver. A delightful collection of stories from out of the Ovando, Montana, and Bob Marshall Wilderness areas in Montana by a noted storyteller, 160 pages, clothbound and softcover editions.*

Mules & Mountains, *By Margie E. Hahn, the story of Walt Hahn, Forest Service Packer, 164 pages, clothbound or softcover editions*

Hunting Books

High Pressure Elk Hunting, *By Mike Lapinski. The latest book available on hunting elk that have become educated to the presence of more hunters working them, 192 pages, many photographs, hardcover or softcover.*

Bugling for Elk, *By Dwight Schuh, the bible on hunting early-season elk. A recognized classic, 164 pages, softcover edition only.*

Coyote Hunting, *By Phil Simonski. Presents basics on hunting coyotes as well as caring for the pelts, 126 pages, many photographs, softcover only.*

Elk Hunting in the Northern Rockies, *By Ed Wolff. Uses expertise of five recognized elk hunting experts to show the five basic concepts used to hunt elk. Another of our very popular books, 162 pages, many photographs.*

So You Really Want To Be a Guide, *By Dan Cherry. The latest and single most authoritative source on what it takes to be a guide today. This book is an excellent guideline to a successful guiding career. Softcover edition only.*

Field Care Handbook For The Hunter & Fisherman, *By Bill Sager & Duncan Gilchrist, 168 pages, comb binding, many photographs and illustrations. The most comprehensive field care handbook available.*

Hunting Open Country Mule Deer, *By Dwight Schuh. Simply the best and most detailed book ever done for getting in close to big mule deer. The ultimate mule deer book by a recognized master, 14 chapters, 180 pages.*

Montana Hunting Guide, *By Dale A. Burk, the most comprehensive and fact-filled guidebook available on hunting in Montana, 192 pages, clothbound or softcover editions.*

Taking Big Bucks, *By Ed Wolff. Subtitled "Solving the Whitetail Riddle," this book presents advice from top whitetail experts with an emphasis on hunting western whitetails. 176 pages, 62 photographs.*

Radical Elk Hunting Strategies, *By Mike Lapinski. Takes over where other books on early-season elk hunting leave off to give advice on what the hunter must do to adapt to changing conditions. 162 pages, 70 photographs.*

Western Hunting Guide, *By Mike Lapinski, the most thorough guide on hunting the western states available. A listing of where-to-go in the western states alone makes the book a valuable reference tool, 168 pages, clothbound or softcover editions.*

STONEYDALE PRESS PUBLISHING COMPANY
523 Main Street • Box 188
Stevensville, Montana 59870
Phone: 406-777-2729